I0157642

Worms

by

Murray Dailey

WingSpan Press

Dedication

To:
Charlotte, Daniel, Olivia, Josephine, Dylan, Madeleine, Catherine, Chase, Jesse, Ana, James, Grace, Emilie, Jack, Noah, Caroline, Jessica, Avielle, Benjamin and Allison.

From Sandy Hook Elementary, Newtown, Connecticut.
Gone too soon but not forgotten.

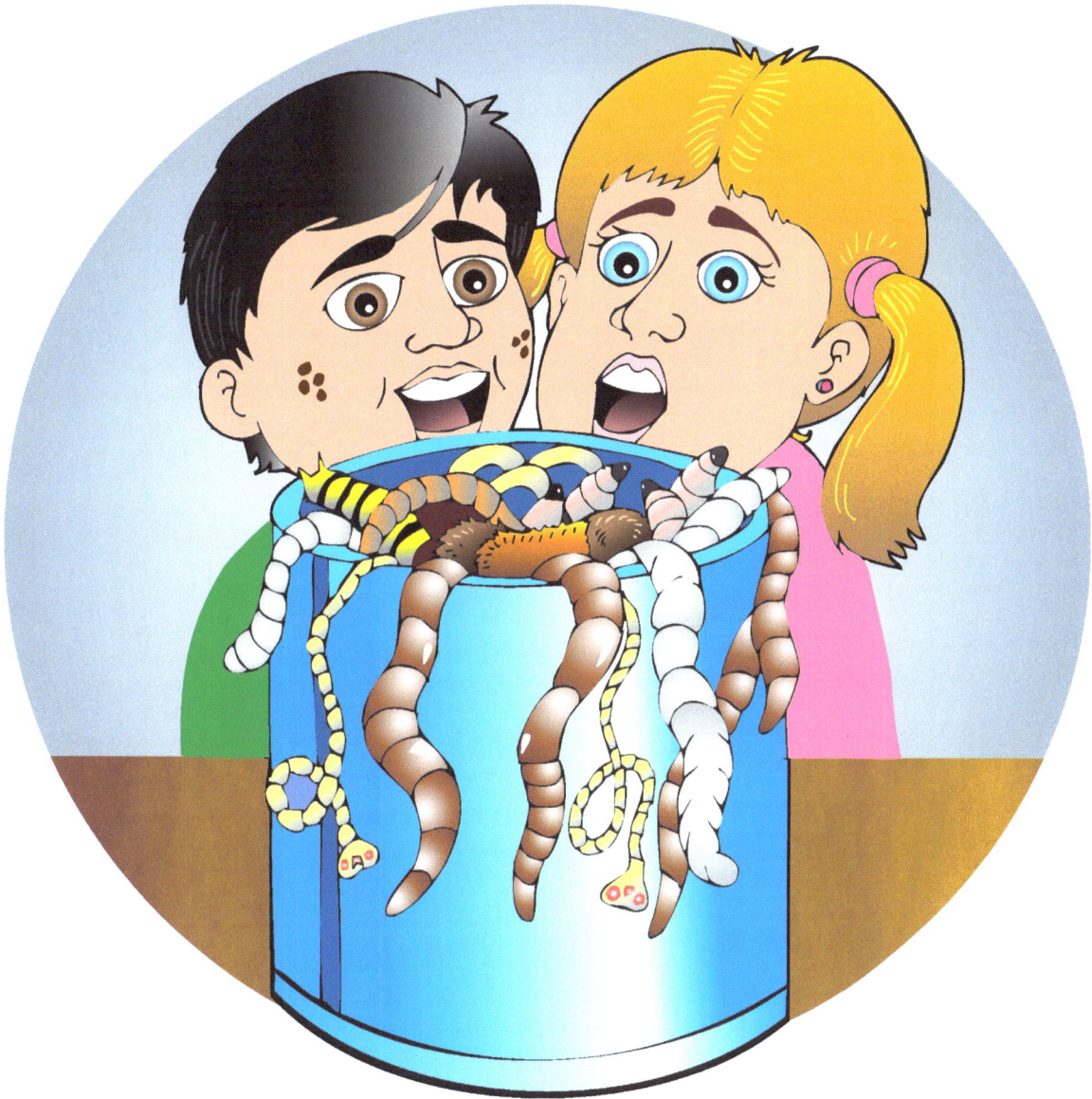

You may think you are not afraid of anything
But there is one thing that gives you the squirms
Looking down into a can of goo
And seeing a bunch of YUCKY WORMS!

Most everybody thinks
Worms are only in the ground

But if you take the time to look
You would be surprised where they can be found

Worms can be fat and fuzzy
You would know them as a caterpillar

They eat up all your lettuce
Then turn into a moth called Miller

Worms are all around us
They can be alone or in a group
You may look down into your bowl
And find them in your soup

Take a worm to school
You could do it on a hunch
That it will be hiding in your box
Waiting on your lunch

Over in an empire named China
Long ago in days of yore
It was worms that spun the cocoon
That made the silk they wore

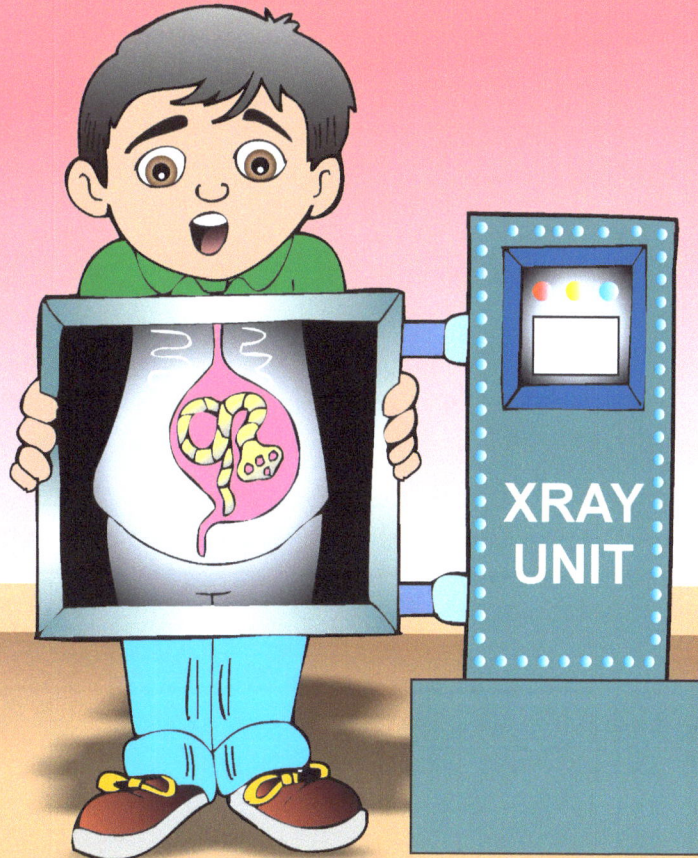

Some worms are long and flat
They are commonly known as tapes
Down inside your small intestine
They are waiting for their mates

When you bite into an apple
You may be at a loss

When you see just half a worm
That was going to be a Codling Moth

When you are husking an ear of corn
Before you begin to chew
You may be surprised to find
That a worm has been there before you

In Africa when your arm or leg has a blister
With something hanging out that is not very thick
It is probably a biblical Guinea Worm
That you have to wind up on a stick

While twisting your pasta to eat
A worm may be hard to see
Because when they are hiding in your dish
They can look just like spaghetti

Some worms are found in water
They could be hiding in your oars
When you see holes in boats and piles
You have found the home of Ship Bores

If you look into a tree
And see worms that loop instead of squirm
You have found a baby Geometer Moth
That begins life known as an Inch Worm

When you are wading in the ocean
You must be careful of your feet
If you step on a stinging fire worm
You have found a Polycheate

When you see tents among the branches
They may look like worms in a silky froth
But if you will wait a while
You will see a Lakey Moth

A worm that lives in dolphins
Is particular where it goes
If eaten by a boy or girl
It may come our their nose

So now you have been introduced
To some of our animal friends known as worms
So the next time you may see one
You may no longer get the SQUIRMS!

Copyright © 2013 by Murray Dailey

All rights reserved.

No part of this book may be reproduced or transmitted in any form or by any means, electronic or mechanical, including photocopying, recording or by any information storage and retrieval system, without written permission from the author, except for the inclusion of brief quotations in review.

Published in the United States and the United Kingdom
by WingSpan Press, Livermore, CA

The WingSpan name, logo and colophon are the trademarks of WingSpan Publishing.

ISBN 978-1-59594-488-7

First edition 2013

Printed in the United States of America

www.wingspanpress.com

Library of Congress Control Number: 2013934465

1 2 3 4 5 6 7 8 9 10

www.ingramcontent.com/pod-product-compliance
Lightning Source LLC
Chambersburg PA
CBHW042114040426
42448CB00002B/263